The Wonder of You

A Book for Celebrating Baby's First Year

Welcome to the world, little one!
You are the one and only ever you!

NANCY TILLMAN

A Feiwel and Friends Book
An Imprint of Macmillan

Library of Congress Cataloging-in-Publication Data Available

ISBN-13: 978-0-312-36839-5
ISBN-10: 0-312-36839-9

Feiwel and Friends logo designed by Filomena Tuosto

First Edition: May 2008

10 9 8 7 6 5 4 3 2 1

www.feiwelandfriends.com

The Wonder of You

A Book for Celebrating Baby's First Year

For: _____

On the night you were born,
the moon smiled with such wonder
that the stars peeked in to see you
and the night wind whispered,
"Life will never be the same."

Because there had never
been anyone like you . . .
ever in the world.

WE WANTED YOU SO MUCH. . . . .

From the moment we knew you were coming, we

_____

_____

_____

_____

_____

_____

_____

How we planned for you_____

_____

_____

_____

_____

_____

_____

_____

We wanted you so much that
we skipped and sang
and told the world till
the heavens rang.

At last our dreams
have all come true . . .
for that's how much
we wanted you.

SHOWERS OF LOVE

Date:_____

Hosted by:_____

People attending:

_____   _____
_____   _____
_____   _____
_____   _____
_____   _____
_____   _____
_____   _____
_____   _____
_____   _____
_____   _____

So enchanted with you

were the wind and the rain

that they whispered the sound

of your wonderful name. . . .

INVITATIONS AND/OR PHOTOS

GIFTS

For you to wear:

_____

_____

_____

_____

For your room:

_____

_____

_____

_____

For us to read to you:

_____

_____

_____

_____

For you to play with:

_____

_____

_____

_____

_____

_____

_____

_____

_____

MIRACLES

S O N O G R A M
O R
P H O T O

Date: _____

OUR FIRST THOUGHTS ABOUT YOU

Where we were when we heard you would at last be ours _____

_____

_____

_____

_____

You are uniquely ours because _____

_____

_____

_____

You delight us because _____

_____

_____

_____

We want you to know that _____

_____

_____

_____

It sailed through the farmlands
high on the breeze. . . .

ADVENTURES IN BRINGING YOU HOME

Your first day home: _____

_____

_____

_____

_____

_____

_____

Your first night home: _____

_____

_____

_____

_____

_____

_____

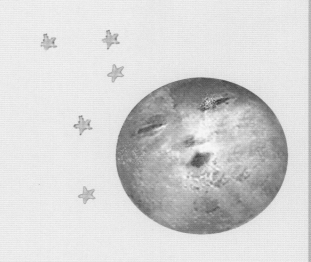

FIRST DAY HOME PHOTOS

PHOTOS

THE ONE AND ONLY EVER YOU!

FIRST PHOTO

Your wonderful name is

We chose your name because

Date and time you were born

Place you were born

Weight and length

Your eyes are a beautiful

Your hair is a gorgeous shade of

BIRTH OR ADOPTION
ANNOUNCEMENT HERE

YOU'RE JUST AN ANGEL. . . .

Dreams we have for you_____

_____

_____

_____

_____

_____

_____

_____

_____

_____

_____

_____

_____

PHOTO

HERE IS A LOCK
OF YOUR HAIR

FAMILY TREE

Great-grandmothers

_____

_____

Great-grandfathers

_____

_____

Grandmother

_____

_____

Grandfather

_____

_____

Your Parent

_____

Brothers & Sisters_____

FAMILY TREE

Great-grandmothers

_____

_____

Great-grandfathers

_____

_____

Grandmother

_____

_____

Grandfather

_____

_____

Your Parent

_____

Brothers & Sisters_____

CELEBRATING YOU
Christening, dedication, bris, or special service

Type of service_____

Service was held at_____

What you wore_____

Who came

_____ _____ _____

_____ _____ _____

_____ _____ _____

_____ _____ _____

_____ _____ _____

_____ _____ _____

Until everyone heard it and everyone knew
of the one and only ever you. . . .

EVERYONE SAYS YOU HUNG THE MOON!

PHOTOS

YOUR FIRST ROOM

PHOTO

Not once had there been such eyes,
such a nose, such silly, wiggly,
wonderful toes. . . .
In fact, I think I'll count to three
so you can wiggle your toes for me!

PHOTOS

OTHER FIRSTS

First smiled_____

First laughed_____

First held your head up_____

First rolled over_____

First sat up_____

PHOTO

First held a bottle_____

First crawled_____

First stood alone_____

First words_____

_____

_____

PHOTO

First steps_____

First slept through the night_____

First ate solid food_____

First fed yourself_____

First babysitter_____

Other firsts_____

_____

_____

_____

_____

_____

_____

_____

FAVORITES

Favorite people _____

Favorite foods _____

Favorite bedtime toy _____

Favorite story _____

Favorite lullaby _____

Favorite playtime activity _____

When the polar bears heard, they danced until dawn. . . .

But I am very displeased when

_____

_____

_____

_____

GLAD YOU  MAD YOU

PHOTO

PHOTO

Glad because:

_____

_____

_____

_____

Mad because:

_____

_____

_____

_____

THE WORLD YOU CAME INTO...

President _____

Trends _____

Hot toys _____

Popular children's books _____

Popular songs _____

Popular movies _____

Popular TV shows _____

Popular clothing styles _____

Other _____

From faraway places,
the geese flew home. . . .

Price of milk _____ movies _____

gasoline _____ diapers _____

Date_____

HANDPRINTS & FOOTPRINTS

Special
Delivery

BETTE DAVIS

USA **42**

2008

PHOTOS OF FIRST HOME

YOUR HEALTH

IMMUNIZATION DETAILS

Vaccine	Age	Date

Hearing test _____

Eyesight test _____

Allergies _____

Blood type _____

Pediatrician _____

Childhood illnesses	Date

TEETHING

First tooth_____

Second tooth_____

Third tooth_____

Favorite teething items_____

_____

_____

_____

☐ It was easy!

☐ It was not!

PHOTO

And none
of the ladybugs
flew away. . . .

FIRST-YEAR LENGTH AND WEIGHT

So whenever you doubt
just how special you are
and you wonder who loves you,
how much and how far,
listen for geese honking
high in the sky.
(They're singing
a song to remember
you by.)

Age	Weight	Length		Age	Weight	Length
1 month				7 months		
2 months				8 months		
3 months				9 months		
4 months				10 months		
5 months				11 months		
6 months				12 months		

Or notice the bears
asleep at the zoo.
(It's because they've been
dancing all night for you!)
Or drift off to sleep to the
sound of the wind.
(Listen closely . . .
it's whispering your name
again!)

PHOTO

PHOTO

AT_____MONTHS

AT_____MONTHS

WE SEE GREAT THINGS FOR YOU. . . . .

Already, your personality shows us that_____

_____

_____

_____

_____

_____

Some of your most special character traits are_____

_____

_____

_____

_____

If the moon stays up
until morning one day,
or a ladybug lands
and decides to stay,
or a little bird sits
at your window awhile,
it's because they're all
hoping to see you smile.

RUB-A-DUB

PHOTO

It's you in the tub!

SPECIAL HOLIDAYS

PHOTOS

PHOTOS

Memories of your favorite holiday

_____

_____

_____

_____

_____

_____

For never before in story or rhyme
(not even once upon a time)
has the world ever known a you, my friend,
and it never will, not ever again.

PHOTOS

WONDERFUL, MARVELOUS YOU. . .

Fabulous

Firsts!

BIRTHDAY PHOTO OR INVITATION

FIRST BIRTHDAY

Theme_____

_____

Location_____

Favorite presents_____

_____

_____

_____

_____

_____

_____

_____

Cake_____

_____

Who attended_____

_____

_____

_____

_____

_____

_____

_____

_____

_____

_____

_____

YOU WERE BORN WITH
A CROWN ON YOUR HEAD.

This year you learned to _____

_____

_____

_____

_____

_____

_____

_____

PHOTO

Your favorite toys are _____

_____

_____

_____

_____

_____

_____

You giggle when_____

_____

_____

_____

_____

You are stubborn if_____

_____

_____

_____

Your playmates are _____

_____

_____

_____

ALLOW US TO TOOT YOUR HORN!

Heaven blew every
trumpet and played
every horn
on the wonderful,
marvelous
night you were born.

PHOTOS

Best 1-year-old stories

PHOTOS

BLESSINGS FROM FRIENDS AND FAMILY

YOU ARE LOVED.